MARC CHAGALL

Jacques Damase is a regular contributor to the most important French art periodicals. His books include monographies on Kijno, Atlan and the sculptor César. He is an intimate friend of the great French painters.

JACQUES DAMASE

Marc Chagall

BLANDFORD PRESS
LONDON

editor: Anthony Bosman
lay-out: Wim van Stek and Aart Verhoeven
photography: Daniel Frasnay, Paris
first published in the English edition in 1963
by Blandford Press Ltd. London
reproduction rights 1963: A.D.A.G.P., Paris
© 1963 and printed in Holland by The Ysel Press Ltd, Deventer

MARC CHAGALL

With the Chagalls, one did not only read the Bible, one lived it. At the family table, just large enough to accommodate the eight sisters and their brother, there was always, on the eve of the Passover, an empty place for the prophet Elija.

The artist's grandfather, a butcher at Lyozna, a village close to Vitebsk, used to spend half his life at home in prayer, and the other half in his shop. He was a very unusual sort of fellow, this grandfather. In one of his pictures Chagall has represented him seated on the roof of his house, enjoying the evening air together with the final dish of his supper.

There was also Uncle Noah, who belonged to the Hassidim, a Russian Jewish sect which at that time was still very powerful and which, in its opposition to asceticism, used to teach the principles of a constant communication between man and God through the medium of a sort of ecstatic joy. A notable personage in the sect, Uncle Noah undoubtedly left his imprint on Marc Chagall. "He carted animals," says the artist in his autobiography, "and I used often to accompany him in his jolting cart. He was a good violinist. He played to me for hours at a time, seated on a step in the back yard, and entertained me with sacred stories. We would escape, both of us, from the sordidness of everyday life and travel in dreams through a marvellous world where the figures of Scripture would assume an authentic reality."

Thus the little boy of Vitebsk, born on July 7, 1887, was at once caught up in a life both highly colourful and productive of strong impressions. Moreover, he himself says, "If my art played no part in the life of my parents, their life and their creations have strongly influenced my art."

He received lessons from an old academic painter at Vitebsk. In 1907, after receiving some advice from Leon Bakst (the famous scene designer for Diaghilev's Russian Ballets)—or, to be more exact, after working for some time in his studio at St. Petersburg, in company with Countess Tolstoi and Nijinsky-Chagall painted one of the first pictures which he cared to remember, "Death". "The hedges of the town once counted," he writes again, "I painted Death. Mother used to supervise my painting. She considered, for example, that in the picture 'Birth', the body of the young mother should be swathed in bandages. I at once complied with her wishes—she was right, the figure came to life. . . . Bella brought me some blue flowers, mixed with green leaves. She was all in white, wearing black gloves; I painted her portrait. . . . Once having felt the pulse of all my family, I painted 'The Wedding'" (the second version of which may be seen on p. 21).

These few notes by the adolescent artist show us indeed his manner of thinking and seeing, and also his subsequent need to escape the sordidness of everyday life, although being always tied to it. The adolescent takes careful note of his surroundings —the men, the peasants' cottages, the open spaces. Reality, poor and chill as it is, at once stimulates and restricts him. It is something which one must pass beyond, so that one may know what is behind it. Curiosity was awakened concerning the mystery in question, first glimpsed under a tragic or grotesque aspect. Already the human figures assume importance at the expense of the landscape; sometimes they are merely marionettes, as we ourselves often are in life: the shrill wail of a violin expresses their undefined suffering.

The official date of his first work is 1907. What did he do before that? He was born and lived as a child in fairly poor circumstances. His father was a simple clerk at a herring warehouse. He suffered in seeing his father suffer. His parents, by dint of hard sacrifices, allowed him to continue his studies. For that, it was necessary to pay fifty roubles to a teacher, for in those days it was very difficult to enter a Jewish child into a state school. Marc Chagall was a good pupil; he used to write poems and, as he was able to sing in tune, he used to earn a few coppers at the synagogue on festival days. Of an evening he would draw. His first portrait was most certainly that of the pianist Rubinstein, copied from an illustrated paper.

The drama was soon to begin: "I feel very much at ease with you all," he writes in *My Life,* "but have you not heard of the traditions, of Aix, of the painter with his ear cut off, of the cubes and squares of Paris?"

In the studio of Bakst he used to obtain the first reproductions of the new French painters, and that gave him the desire to get a closer look at this art. And so, in 1910, the artist came to Paris, thanks to a small amount of money granted to him by a patron at St. Petersburg. He soon installed himself at "La Ruche" (The Hive). This was the name given to some hundred studios surrounded by small gardens close to the slaughterhouses of Vaugirard. These studios were inhabited by bohemian artists from all countries.

"While in the Russian studios an offended model would be sobbing, and from the Italians would arise songs and the sound of the guitar, and from the Jews, arguments, I would be alone in my studio, before my oil lamp. A studio piled up with pictures, and with canvases, which actually were not canvases but my towels, sheets, and nightshirts cut in pieces. . . . At two or three o'clock in the morning the sky would be blue and the dawn approaching. Not far off, cattle were being slaughtered, cows were lowing, and I would paint them."

That year he painted "The Studio" (p. 19), which actually anticipated Soutine, for Soutine had not yet done anything in that genre, so that this picture, both in regard to its technique and historically, is of tremendous importance.

Later, Soutine was also to live at the Hive, where he would often come back from the market with two or three rotting fowl, in order to paint them. Modigliani would come back dead drunk, banging at Chagall's door and asking: "I bet you are still painting your cows, aren't you?"

"Thus I used to sit up every night," adds the master. "The studio had not been cleaned up for a week. Canvas stretchers, egg shells, empty tins of cheap soup would be strewn about everywhere. My lamp would burn, and I with it. It would burn until its brightness grew dim in the blue of the morning. It was then that I would climb into my garret. . . . On the floor would be, side by side, reproductions of El Greco and Cézanne and the remains of a herring which I would divide into two parts, the head for one day and the tail for the next, and, thank God, some crusts of bread. . . . Before entering my studio people always had to wait so as to give me time to tidy up, to dress myself, for I used to work nude. In general, I could not endure a garment of any kind; I disliked putting on clothes, and dressed in a slovenly manner. . . . Nobody bought any of my pictures. I had scarcely thought of that as a possibility."

And he continues to show us the Paris he knew before the First World War: "More than once, in my search for art, I would wander down the Rue Lafitte, contemplating hundreds of Renoirs, Pissarros, and Monets at Durand-Ruel's. Vollard's shop used particularly to attract me, but I did not dare enter it. In its dark and dusty windows there was nothing but old newspapers and a small carved figure by Maillol which looked as if it had strayed there by mistake. I looked for the Cézannes; they were on the wall at the back, unframed. I pressed myself against the shop window, flattening my nose; then all at once I would catch sight of Vollard himself. He was alone in the middle of his shop, wearing an overcoat. I was afraid to go in. He looked surly. I dared not. . . .

"But at Bernheim's, on the Place de la Madeleine, the shop windows were lighted up as if for a wedding. . . . There were Van Goghs, Gauguins, Matisses. . . . You could look, enter, and leave as you pleased. That was what I used to do, once or twice a week. It was at the Louvre that I felt most at home.

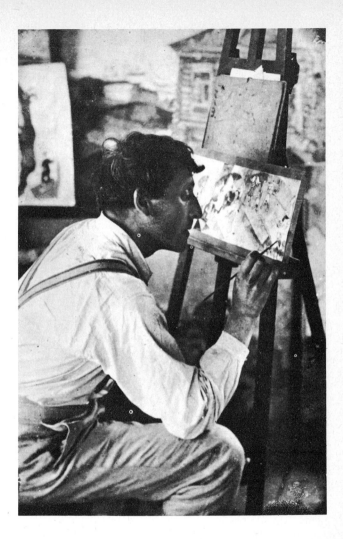

Marc Chagall at the end of the First World War.

Long-lost friends were there. Their prayers were my own, and their pictures caused my young face to shine. Rembrandt used to captivate me. Chardin, Fouquet, Gericault stopped me more than once. . . ."

Glorious epoch! It was then that he met Blaise Cendrars, with whom he formed a close friendship, Canudo, Max Jacob, André Salmon, La Fresnaye, Delaunay, also Apollinaire, who frightened him a little, for Apollinaire was the embodiment of cubism. But Apollinaire liked his works, murmured "Supernatural!" and introduced him to Walden, who organised, in Berlin in 1914, his first one-man exhibition, on the premises of the review *Der Sturm*. From this visit with Apollinaire and from their subsequent relationship was to originate one of the finest pictures painted by Chagall during the year 1911-12, "Homage to Apollinaire" (p. 20), a picture in keeping, moreover, with the theories to be utilized later by Robert Delaunay. For the exhibition in Berlin, Chagall sent two hundred paintings and numerous gouaches, which were destined to remain stacked up there at the declaration of war. But the painter had a desire to see his homeland, Russia, once more, and he passed through Berlin just to look at his exhibition and then made his way to Vitebsk.

There he found Bella, to whom he had long been betrothed, and married her. War broke out and he was called up. In 1917 came the Revolution. Chagall, who had been appointed Commissioner for Fine Arts for the town of Vitebsk, founded an academy and had his works copied by the artists of the town. On the occasion of the first anniversary of the October Revolution, in 1919 Granowsky, the Director of the Jewish Theatre in Moscow, asked him for frescoes for the theatre and its foyer, and he worked at these. Chagall invited Lissitzky, Malevitch, and Pougny to come and teach in his academy at Vitebsk.

In 1922 Chagall had just left Russia for good; he was in Berlin with his wife and small daughter, where, since his exhibition in 1914, he had become in the eyes of the Germans one of the masters of expressionism. He gained glory but no money; as far as market value went, it was thought that glory should be enough for him! During his time in the German capital, the artist was to become familiar with the techniques of graphic art, which were destined to become the means of developing one of his favourite modes of expression.

In 1923 Chagall settled in Paris, still accompanied by his wife and their little Ida, in a studio on the Avenue d'Orleans. By that time he had long been in full control of his medium of expression and his work already included a number of masterpieces.

His first series of etchings, intended to illustrate his autobiography, *My Life,* was published in Berlin by Cassirer. His friend Cendrars at last introduced him to Vollard, whom he had never dared to approach, but who, with his usual flair, immediately ordered from him 96 etchings as illustrations for Gogol's poetic novel *Dead Souls* (pp. 39, 41, 45, 46, 48, 56). He worked at these until 1927, and then began, immediately afterwards, the 100 illustrations for La Fontaine's *Fables* (pp. 49-54), work which lasted three years. In 1931 he undertook a journey to the Middle East for the purpose of rediscovering the atmosphere of the Bible, which he wanted to illustrate, again for Vollard. We shall return to this later, since the Bible was not completed at the death of Vollard, its intended publisher; for other reasons, too, these three books did not appear until after 1945, under the imprint of Teriade.

In the meantime, Chagall had already had a retrospective exhibition, also his first exhibitions in New York and Basel.

After this brief glimpse of the early background and first steps of the artist, let us now watch his work develop.

A man asleep, and a child whose faculties of imagination and creativity are not yet hampered by the restrictions of the conventions, may acquiesce in marvels and mysteries, such as the master Chagall has shown us. As for the man asleep: in that state he would seem to be more intelligent than when he is

11

awake, since he will accept in sleep things at which he would laugh on waking up—things that he laughs at in order to conceal from himself the fact that they disturb him.

An instinctive painter, Chagall is a free man; he paints what pleases him, and always, miraculously deliberate. Compositions seemingly the most impossible, the most far-fetched, the most daring, the most absurd, appear in his work as natural and normal. We are in the world of dreams, and in that world the most unexpected things happen to us, without for one moment astonishing us.

Let us go back to 1912 and look at that admirable painting, "Self-portrait with Seven Fingers" (p. 22). Everything is there—one of his first Eiffel Towers, on the easel the sketch entitled "To Russia, with Donkeys and Others", which the painter explains thus: "For me a painting is a surface covered with objects depicted in a certain order. For example, the headless woman, who, with a milk pail, figures on this canvas—if I had the idea of separating her head from her body it was because I needed a space just at that spot."

Surrealism, which at that time Apollinaire was still referring to merely as "supernatural", had already arrived. This we see, years in advance of Paul Klee, in "Man in the Snow" (p. 24)—to the left, the entire sky red, in squares like a draughtboard, with the round, moonlike face in it—a perfect Paul Klee!

Having reached the limits of all the schools—surrealism, expressionism, Orphism, cubism, Fauvism, and all the other "isms"—and also the limits of the poets' world, Chagall, more than any other contemporary painter, although frequently a precursor, discoverer, and an extraordinary inventor, has always been able to hold us and to draw us into his unique world. This artist's exceptional power, his personality, can at no period in his life be confused with that of any other artist.

Attempts have often been made to place this painter in all the categories of modern art, but never with any success: he is beyond classification, beyond measure, beyond family back-

Marc Chagall giving painting lessons during the Russian Revolution

ground, beyond competition, beyond genre. His genre is his own entirely, and he is constantly renewing himself.

"I don't want to be the same as all the others, I want to discover a new world," Chagall used to say in his youth, and he saw the fulfillment of this wish.

"By way of response," he continues, "the town seemed to snap like the strings of a violin, and all the inhabitants started walking on air, leaving their habitual locations. Familiar personages installed themselves on the roofs and rested there. All the colours were upset and turned into wine, so that liquor gushes from my canvases—as, for example, in the 'Double Portrait with the Glass of Wine' or in that of 'The Red Horse' " (p. 59). How is it possible to explain in a finer and more beautiful manner his way of seeing and feeling?

An eye-witness in 1928 describes the painter as follows: "We were in a café. Chagall was wearing a yellow shirt with a black collar. While talking, he absent-mindedly drank his coffee. He was, as they say, not there—gone to another world where the landscapes, to judge from his expression, seemed to be of a nostalgic character. While expressing himself Chagall had several faces.

I have seen him curled up tightly like a cat, pointed like a shrew-mouse, motionless like an owl—his body I do not remember very well—the whole of him was concentrated in his head."

This description is sufficiently accurate and may serve as the explanation of a certain canvas concerning which Chagall said in reply to questions about it. "In 'The Village and I' I have depicted a small cow and a milkmaid in the head of a large cow, because I needed this for my composition as I conceived of it, in regard to form and genre at that particular place." It is an almost Cartesian explanation, one point summing up the whole.

This baffling genius, with a passionate and intoxicating attach-ment to poetry, and careful to preserve for his pictures a rich-ness of form at the same time as the vibration of the original

14

emotion, would reply in this way to the questions posed.

For the sensitivity of Chagall, as another critic has pointed out, was purely emotional and not literary. And if he was a poet, and a great poet, he has ignored entirely the "literary" aspect of poetry. His sublime phrases were not planned compositions, but visions: the "Street of Lyozna by Day" had resuscitated the art of Masaccio and of Piero della Francesca. Speaking of his aunts he said, "Winged like angels, they would fly across the market place, over the baskets of berries, pears, and gooseberries. People would look at them and ask: 'Whoever can fly about like that?'" This shows the simplicity with which he would always explain the most extraordinary things, which were his daily bread.

We have been drawn by him into a universe in movement. *Chagall* in Russian means "to go fast". Chagall was a man who never ceased to move forward. But these long journeys did not take place by road or by aeroplane; they were accomplished in his head and on the canvas.

When one surveys the works of Chagall in the different periods, one is rarely conscious of any change in the essential tone; the same atmosphere of intimacy is found in all this work, as in the delicate and touching "Mother at the Stove" (p. 23). Mass emigrations pained him. One can sense that in "The Soldiers" and "The Old Man" which show one, more effectually than a thousand discourses, the stupidity of war and the misery of the old man fleeing from his home (pp. 25, 26). What strikes one forcibly in his work is, indeed, its directness; in one way or another he speaks directly to you. "What is more", adds Jean Grenier, "he always takes part in the scene; he sees himself as living in it and sees you as living in it; he hears you speak and hears himself speak; this dual interchange goes on all the time, it is a game into which he draws his interlocutor—a game in which laughter is close to tears, seriousness to frivolity, and self-conceit to self-forgetfulness."

"The Lovers in Green" (p. 27) depicts the beauty of love and confides to you the secret of the lovers' universe. These two figures in red and white perform no action; they pursue their dream, but they compel you to share it. His inspirations dating from that period express universal tenderness, an ability to apprehend the inner life of people; the picture is painted from within. In the same way, one can also appreciate "The Lovers in Blue" (p. 31).

"What am I?" Chagall exclaims (mezza voce). "Nothing—I see nothing in myself. Am I a celebrity? They say I am, but look at me, I am *not* a celebrity. I look ; I see a man despoiled of his renown and he does not deserve any better. . ."

Chagall, when one meets him, either at his flat overlooking the banks of the Ile St. Louis in Paris, or at his country estate in Vence, looks like a schoolboy on holiday, or, if he is not working, like a schoolboy playing tag or playing truant.

Quickly he leaves you, however, and retires into his "world", where he transforms "into visual sensations the most subtle nuances within his soul."

For him it is not a question of breaking up the essence of the landscape, as with the impressionists, by decomposing the light (actually, landscape does not interest him from that point of view—except the landscape at Montchauvet (p. 30)— landscape is for him a medium of evocation, a scenic background rather than a thing-in-itself). Nor is it a question of systematically demolishing the structure of things, as with the cubists: "He is only interested in leading us to the inside, to the centre of the intricate machinery of the heart and the spirit."

These liberties of the imagination, of the heart and spirit, are, however, made subject to the laws of rhythm and balance; they assume, so to speak, architectural outlines.

And if he makes use of reality he always transforms it, and transposes it, so that it is seen almost entirely through his imagination. His most idealized figures certainly testify to the fact that nature has been carefully consulted. But Chagall "knows how to extract from a person not only his dream-potential but also the physical mass which he represents and the place which he occupies."

Conventions are upset; he upsets conventions and transforms living beings; these personages undergo a total metamorphosis. Witchcraft holds sway in a supernatural atmosphere, where life with its magical qualities remains forever constant, where the rationale of conventional experience is abolished. We are placed before the beam of a magic lantern coming from no one knows where. And even in the gloomiest pictures there is a kind of festive air about things.

He plays amazing tricks on us. Chagall places his objects in a fantastic and supernatural setting and changes their colours. He is, or was occasionally, especially in his early works, haunted by inner dreams, upon which memory images became engrafted. But from his memories, combined or juxtaposed, he derives powerful effects of strangeness, of irony, an impression both acute and profound. He takes them out of their setting, renders them anachronistic; he deprives people of their heads, which they replace themselves—often upside down. Sometimes this reverse arrangement is a sign of ecstasy or of uncertainty, or of complete aberration. A poet with his head reversed, or a painter (p. 32), expresses a popular attitude, does it not? So why be astonished at it? At times one becomes only too much aware of the sadness which such a thing represents.

Thus the eye of the painter embroiders around humble realities the patterns of a new mythology, expressed in delicate arabesques and colours of subtle fluorescence, which spatter you with their miraculous draught of fishes, so that after you have seen these images their reflections remain in your eyes and heart.

There is richness too; an extraordinary lightness with the brush enables Chagall to enrich the entire tone of a multitude of high lights by making them reinforce one another by almost imperceptible caresses.

He plays like a juggler with colours and objects—balls, skittles, clocks, heads, candlesticks, things of every description.

17

An intrepid performer, he performs without a safety net, yet his skill never fails him; he is the Rastelli, the perfect master, of the arabesque and of colour.

"It might be said," Chagall says, "that while still in my mother's womb I had become aware of the purity of the colours of flowers, and that when I first saw a young girl I was dazzled by her beauty... though without any feelings of sex. I was dazzled by purity in all things. This purity I failed to discover in my paintings in my own surroundings. It was in search of this purity that I left Vitebsk for St. Petersburg, and St. Petersburg for Paris. ....I do not know whether colour chose me or whether I chose colour, but since my childhood I have been wedded to purity of colour, and nothing which I was taught ever satisfied me."

If we realize that he is as much in love with life as with his painting, that may explain what he means by "chemistry".

For drawing itself is often limited to certain attitudes, objects, or types arrested once for always (as with a betrothed pair who embrace amid flowers, flying clocks, and fabulous beasts) but which are transfigured by a riot of colour such as succeeds in reconciling the most incompatible tones and in creating a supernatural setting, made up less of profound emotions and gravity (as with Bosch, El Greco, Ensor, and Redon) than of a chemical mystery—to quote a favourite expression of the poet's.

"Theory," he says, "and technique have not enabled me to advance one step; I owe everything to life. Painting is not a matter of the schools; it is above all a species of chemistry. I have suggested that one day an exhibition be set up of pictures, abstract or otherwise, shown upside down, so that the blood, the chemistry, may be seen. ... Look at this tree; it is chemically perfect. This plant, those flowers, move me because they are perfect. One is stirred only by that which is perfect: Mozart, Rembrandt."

An attempted explanation of Chagall's "chemistry" is given by a journalist, who explains it as the meeting of unreality

18

(continued on page 73)

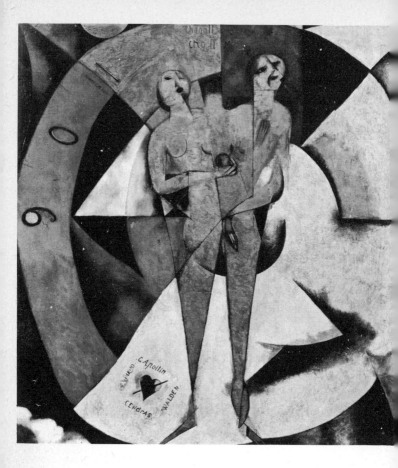

Chagall 1914

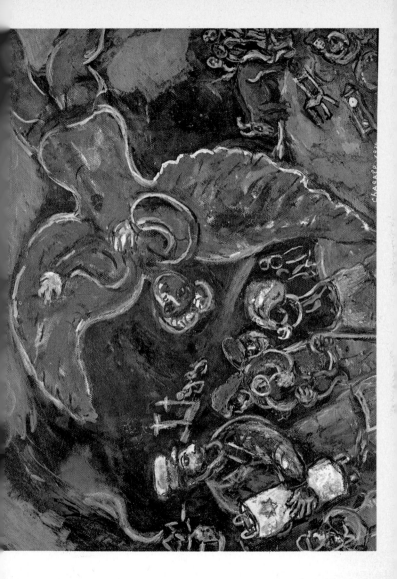

41

רייַזק
דער
מעלאַמעד

44

with matter, the fusion of the unlike elements which make up man—and the world—with the image of these which the painter creates.

Thus it is necessary to speak of matter even where his paintings are concerned, i.e., of what he calls "chemistry". "There can be no great textural work without chemistry," he has occasionally explained. "One can be very intelligent, very clever, and have no chemistry. . . and then one is not a painter. Titian, on the other hand—what chemistry! That is why Titian has been likened to a stream of creative imagination. An example among the moderns is Franz Marc, with his freedom, as shown in his 'Wind in the Fields'; he not only has ideas, he also has chemistry."

I was thinking of this chemistry the other day, at Amsterdam, before Rembrandt's "Man Wearing a Turban", in which the white of this turban impresses you immediately, like a lighthouse lighting the whole room. It seemed to me impossible that a white object should dazzle thus, and I thought of other white pictures which seem so dead, as if covered with ashes— as with certain abstract painters. Rembrandt's white is alive, like the colours of Chagall. One can feel the blood coursing under the skin, and a heart which beats and will never cease to beat. If Chagall calls that "chemistry", I should be inclined to call it a miracle, or magic, the magic of organic, fluid matter which cannot be explained any more than one can explain why some men are seers or mediums, and others have no such faculty.

After his arrival in Paris he found all that he had been seeking, this light and freedom which he had met nowhere else: "I lived as if in a bath of colour. I was enraptured. I knew that I could work in this light and that my dreams would take shape in it. I was overwhelmed by it all. When I saw Seurat I was dazzled. . . . When I saw Monet I could have wept. It was so pure."

Purity forms part of his deepest sentiments, as do poetry, tenderness, and irony.

We have a vision of worlds and of sentiments which we cannot discover in ourselves. We have scales before our eyes which must be removed, and the painter will take charge of this for us. Chagall is our twentieth-century Watteau.

Chagall, as Paul Fierens wrote, is the painter of the kiss; he is also the painter of *fêtes galantes*. He clothes in bright colours this dusty and anxious old world, in which many a person is not sure of being able for long to keep his head on his shoulders!

Certain people—with complete disregard for logic—have in the past refused to admit his principles, since they would not admit that persons painted in a picture could have the appearance of flying. One might reply to them, firstly, that it is the mind which flies and not the persons, and, secondly, that these same people have doubtless seen in all the pictures and ceilings of Tiepolo, Rubens, and El Greco, in all the baroque churches of the seventeenth and eighteenth centuries, angels by the thousands—angels, indeed, only in name, but who could fly without any ado! And this they considered natural!

A painter of the fantastic, of the poetry and mystery of life, an accomplished acrobat and gymnast, he walks on his hands with a book by Gogol, by Chekhov, or with a fable by good old La Fontaine between his teeth; one would perhaps have to imagine these three authors as united together in order to depict him correctly.

Sad at one moment, he becomes optimistic again at the next, and all at once the paint flows onto his canvas like spring rain upon one's head.

An acrobat is shown carrying a town, an entire town, in a balloon; a man is conveying a lighted stove, conveying heat, i.e., love. If I dared, I should say that basically Chagall is the painter of great symbols, but I have an idea that he does not like symbols; he is, moreover, a species of angelic devil (since his devils have white wings). One particular devil is carrying an enormous bouquet of flowers, but one does not know to whom they will be offered—that being the ambiguity both of the picture and of life. The master calls this simply "Harlequinade", but it is much more than that. Modestly, as ever, he conceals under pleasant and frivolous titles the joy and anguish of living.

Chagall, like every man, every artist, becomes obsessed by certain specific themes, which he often repeats, though transposing them, for—I repeat—one must see in his work, *not* the cow, the clock, or the bride, but the essence of all these, and their relationship to each other. The timepiece and the bride introduced into another picture will certainly not be the same, since the setting will have changed; these objects, these beings will never again have the same significance.

Let us not be obsessed by the theme, but by that which it conceals, or shows only in part, or perhaps at a distance—by that which lies behind, is suggested or evoked, rather than by what is shown.

We know of numerous circus paintings by Chagall (pp. 33, 61, 69). I doubt that the master goes often to the circus these days, yet it is a theme which frequently recurs in his work. What, then, does the circus represent for this painter? There is much indeed in this theme which touches upon subjects dear to the artist. The acrobats, the dangerous acts, seemingly impossible and illogical, are just what suit him. The musicians do so, too, as he declares: "I like those musicians hired at weddings, with the sounds of the violins and their harsh waltzes". One feels that he has a tenderness for these strangers, these nameless persons, engaged to amuse us, but who are often the pantomime figures of our own lives.

"And then, who is not a clown," says Chagall to me, "even without a hat? Many people make their own circus and so they have no need to go there. And the colour is as tragic as the circus. . . ."

Plumes on their heads, their hoofs gilded, their rumps decked out with elaborate embroidery, escorted by a glittering equestrienne—he shows us the sentimental life of circus horses—those maned ballerinas—and of their riders. He shows us the young men arrayed, womanlike, in mauve and pale-yellow satin. He shows us circuses from the belvedere where the orchestra is placed to the coliseum tiers, with their successive curves of mandarins' stalls, surmounted by elliptical formations, and, higher up, the vaulted ceiling, tarnished and smoke-grimed, from which drop, like dancing pieces of nickel, ropes, flying trapezes, and other accessories of some act.

One cannot understand the art of Marc Chagall, as Julien Cain has pointed out, without having first understood his infinitely complex personality and having followed him through his life, so rich in adventure. We will note a few of his essential characteristics: fidelity to Biblical tradition and to the religion of his youth; attachment to humble people in small towns, whose customs and strange folklore he has observed; a vibrant sensitivity, always alert, which, when the curtain of mistrust and the mask of irony have been lifted, is revealed as a ceaselessly renewed eruption of enthusiasm for the living creatures, the objects, and the universe which surround him.

Chagall's art is made up of all this. If at first it appears to be unreal, because the dream element predominates, one soon perceives all that has been contributed to it by living experience, observation of the world, and the reading of great books. No art is less abstract than his.

He has invented an animal world of his own. He has within his reach and at his disposition an enchanted realm of animals more extraordinary than any in the loveliest fables or the most beautiful mythology in the world.

There are cocks (p. 60), sometimes cruel, sometimes charming, which strut or bristle, and which end up now as a lady, now as a bouquet of flowers, now as a burst of fireworks. Sometimes too the cocks are as large as horses so that people mount them in order to advance further along the path of happiness and dream (p. 36).

He has invented fishes which, unlike their kind, have decided that it is possible to swim in the sky. A fish, like Jonah's whale, can also be lived in, can hold in its belly a town with a church steeple and a crucifix enclosed in a clock, i.e., within *time*. It can also belong to the category not of catfish, but of womanfish.

And then there are donkeys, goats, small flying horses (p. 59), or farm mules, which lend themselves to every caprice—and the painter is indeed capricious!

When I spoke just now of cocks I should have found another qualifying adjective for them. I used the word "cock" for convenience, but it is in truth a Chagall-bird and one should note that it bears more relationship to its master than to the race of feathered fowl.

In 1935 he travelled in Poland. Between 1936 and 1939, "profoundly disturbed by the threat of war and by the persecutions of his race", he painted dramatic works, notably "Crusifixions" and "The Fall of the Angel" (p. 35).

Here we touch upon another aspect of the master's work, wherein greatness and the element of tragedy frequently surpass the efforts of another great painter, Georges Rouault; the "Crucifixions" of Chagall are more powerful than those of Rouault.

It seems that the further Chagall advances in his work the more he loses, if I may say so, his egocentricity, his concern with "I". If war pictures such as those on pages 55 and 57 will always reflect the anguish and horror experienced by all humanity, this is still through the medium of his own personal sufferings. To-day, however, he appears to be sublimated, no longer interested in his own ego, so that he has attained in his stained glass windows for Jerusalem, for example, and in his recent canvases, such as "The Canticles", a vision of the world truly spiritualized and humanized to such an extent that it is no longer his own portrait that he is painting, but actually that of humanity.

Chagall is certainly a great mystic. "Yes," he replies, "I am a mystic. I do not go to any particular church or synagogue. My prayer is my work. And then I read both Verlaine and the

Bible. I believe in the prophets. Those are my rules of religious observance."

He is above all a mystic in that he is able to blend the human and the supernatural. Moreover, the need for meditation, for renewed self-testing, has been constant with him at all stages of his life.

Let us revert to "his" Bible, to that enterprise which he undertook, thanks to Vollard, but which never saw the light of day until much later, in 1948. None has surpassed him in depicting particular or universal situations. They are, I think, the most beautiful illustrations of the Bible that have ever existed.

Whether he is showing us kings or prophets, women of the people or warriors, he attains the sublime.

On seeing King David weeping before the towers of the city (p. 64), one is deeply moved. The towers of these castles and fortresses are immense constructions suggestive of solitude, so aptly depicted in that terrible picture of 1912.

The great themes of the Bible which he chose to treat are the great themes inherent in man himself. There is much love, as in all his pictures and in all love stories: gay loves, sad loves, memories, reminiscences of love; above all, there is woman—eternal—and man (who was formerly often none other than the artist himself), and there are birth, death, marriage, and burial. "He shows," as Gaston Bachelard so well expresses it, "beings of a primeval life; he revives for us that great of primordial stillness when living beings were born and grew up as a higher form of life. And he projects light and splendour upon everything." The eroticism of Chagall is not like the eroticism of an expressionist such as George Grosz (who seems to have taken much, as did many Germans, from *My Life*); it is the eroticism in its essence, as hallowed in the Bible.

Over and above eroticism, however, we always find in Chagall's work both love and sensuality—the sensuality inherent in matter, in chemistry, and in images.

From 1911 onwards Chagall had begun to treat the theme of

betrothed couples or pairs of lovers—i.e., two figures embracing—which we find continuously throughout his work (pp. 27, 31, 36, 59), gazing into each other's eyes, oblivious to the world around, of which the painter alone is aware. And that theme is natural, since the poet himself was always falling in love. He was a timid lover, not daring to make his proposal, in the case of Bella, but a confident lover in the case of Vava, his second wife. It was for that reason that he was so well able to illustrate *Daphnis and Chloe.*

For *Daphnis and Chloe* he travelled to Greece in search of atmosphere for his characters—of atmosphere only, not reality. He did not want that. Thus his *Daphnis,* one of his latest books, brings us an unreal Greece—though truer than nature—and all the freshness, the enchantment of awakening love—a hymn to love.

His Gogol, with the latter's illogical logic, or rather his logical illogic, at once tragic and amusing, is also extremely sensual. The illustrations for La Fontaine's *Fables,* on the contrary, are—as one would expect—more dry, the technique is different. They constitute a transition stage, leading us to the engravings for the Bible; and the subject, moralising, so French and classical, is viewed with a blending of naturalness, poetry, and philosophy which is enchanting.

In the field of engravings, Chagall's work is immense, outstanding, monumental. Some of his etchings, like Rembrandt's, have that sensitiveness, that feeling of supernormal light, as well as that quality of apparent hesitancy, confused and yet so decisive. What would otherwise be ponderous, with him is transformed miraculously into lightness; it is both heavy and light in the manner of a wave breaking in from the high seas.

In 1941 the Museum of Modern Art in New York invited the artist to take refuge in the United States, where he was to stay all through the war, living a retired life, working in the country. In 1944 he experienced the grief of losing Bella (p. 29), and this was a very sombre period insofar as his work was concerned.

Fortunately Léonide Massine, the choreographer, gave him an order for the scenery and costumes of a new ballet, *Aleko*. For this Chagall was obliged to journey to Mexico, and the trip proved for him to be a startling revelation of colour. "His colours assumed a brilliancy such as they had never had; his paintings acquired a greater relief; the rhythm of his compositions increased in fantasy and daring." Two years later, he worked for a new production of Stravinsky's *Fire Bird*. His last ballet work—the decor and costumes for the revival of Ravel's *Daphnis and Chloe* at the Paris Opera—was a magnificent achievement.

In 1946, the Museum of Modern Art in New York arranged a large retrospective exhibition of his works, and finally, in 1947, he returned to France.

One of his first notable exhibitions in France after the war was to have as its theme: Paris. Paris, which he now loved as his second birthplace and to which he was paying homage. Long before the war he had been in the habit of inserting the Eiffel Tower into his compositions. In 1936 he had painted that wonderful "Bride and Groom of the Eiffel Tower" (p. 36). This time, however, the tower itself, the Place de la Concorde, Notre Dame, the Arc de Triomphe were to be the central figures, as also the Seine. It is the finest homage that Chagall could have given us (pp. 63, 65, 67). In "The Red Roofs" (p. 66) he paid tribute to the city and also united Vitebsk and Paris in marriage. He was having recourse to a very ancient manner of self-expression: a species of picture including the donor—he himself being the donor, the painter in the picture rendering obeisance to the two cities, his two mothers.

Returning to France after the war, he said: "After the American period, I felt a romantic thrill at seeing a Paris again animated and bright after the terrible years that the world had been through."

We now come to another very important stage in his work, the discovery of the stained glass window, which would not have been possible except in France.

A recent photograph of Marc Chagall, taken by
Daniel Frasnay

Certain ancient stained glass windows of Metz Cathedral having been destroyed, it was proposed that he should design some new windows to give light once more to that great church. Chagall went to Chartres, discovered on certain panes of glass, animal figures resembling his own, and had a flash of inspiration concerning that colour-light which he had been seeking. "I could not help thinking," he said, "that only this free natural light, more luminous than any kind of artificial light, can give birth to scintillating canvases on which the revolutions in technique ought to be as natural as the manner of speech, the gesture, and the work of the man in the street."

Moses receiving the Tables of the Law, David and Bathsheba, Jeremiah and the Exodus, an angel sounding a trumpet, a Christ surrounded by symbolic signs — those were the subjects which he chose to depict within the lead-encircled framing of the lancets and rose-windows of Metz.

For the windows intended for a synagogue in Jerusalem another problem arose, since the Jewish religion forbids the portrayal of the human figure. The master decided to depict the twelve tribes of Israel.

He made use of his sacred bestiary — his fishes and winged horses — also his magic and cosmic "objects", characteristic candlesticks, the Tables of the Law, flowers, etc. (see "The Tribe of Reuben", p. 72). And he succeeded in producing the great masterpiece of stained glass windows in modern times. He used, moreover, a system of composition which was unavoidable in view of his technique of breaking up into small pieces the different elements of the picture to join them again by means of strips of lead, which had to be achieved with a light touch by the introduction of slightly geometric compositions into the structures represented, as in the "Homage to Apollinaire" (p. 20).

He achieved, without the use of figures, a work of majesty, just as in his "Crucifixions", especially the "White Crucifixion" of 1938, which is one of his most significant works. "When he showed us this picture for the first time," wrote the late Raissa Maritain, "he did so with a kind of solemnity which was rare with him, and with a profound feeling concerning the importance of the work." Perhaps without thinking, but with a truly unerring instinct, Chagall has shown, in each of his pictures on Christian subjects, the indissoluble union between the two Testaments: the Old announcing the New, and the New fulfilling the Old.

Chagall is one of the greatest painters of our time, since his work always bears a relationship to man, to his feelings—and he knows how to render these feelings—which is rare—not, as in the romantic portrayals by Ingres or Delacroix, with feeling expressed in an anecdote or by means of an exaggerated lyrical outburst—but by showing the fruit of such feelings. And he is able to express in his painting such things as cold, heat, noise, silence. Moreover, he always feels the need to undertake something still greater and more amazing. The need to undertake, at this very moment, gigantic pictures like the last "Canticles", which are like immense frescoes depicting his thought, his feeling, for humanity. These frescoes are intended to adorn, it would seem, some kind of spiritual edifice—not a church, temple, or synagogue—but something which might include all of these and in which the spirit would be free of religious convention. This would be the consummation of what he has been seeking ever since he first handled a paintbrush.

"For my part," he stated in a recent interview, "I have never either sought, nor cared for, realism. When I came to Paris I did not adhere to the cubist movement, which was then at its height; I sought some other movement. The bottle, the guitar, cubes, cylinders—all these represented reality of various kinds. My pictures were illogical and unrealistic. Long before surrealism, what I was looking for was a realism—if you like—but a realism of the soul, something entirely different from a realism dependent on objectivity of geometrical form."

If he paints flowers, for instance, they, like those of Odilon

83

Redon, are no longer simple, natural bouquets, but forests of ideas and spellweaving thoughts, fireworks let off by the painter (p. 34). "I shall be satisfied if you recognise—yourself or other friends—that there lies in the flowers that I paint a subtle spell which makes them akin to the flowers of God. Yes, I should be satisfied if you would recognise this."

Nobody has known better than he how to mingle and to divide the plant and the heavenly kingdoms, the human and the divine, the human and the animal. Nobody except, perhaps, Hieronymus Bosch, how to gauge the proportion of the human and the animal, and the proportion also, of the fantastic, which is to be found in every human being. But what Bosch obtained by terror, Chagall has obtained by gentleness.

He makes use of that marvellous illogic of fairy tales, which makes everything understandable. Everything becomes possible. His forms—women, birds, fishes, animals—with four legs or two—swim in the joy of living and in the sky, with more grace and elegance than the angels or the women of that other great poet, William Blake.

Painter of dreams, Chagall has said: "As for myself, I slept very well without Freud."

Painter of poetic themes, he has said: "Poetry? As an afterthought, yes. I do not seek it; it comes of itself. It is the result of different factors."

Painter of reality, he has said: "The inner world can be more real than the world of appearances. When we dismiss as absurd that which does not seem to us to be logical, we merely prove that we know nothing about nature."

Blaise Cendrars, his great friend, wrote concerning him:
"He takes a church and paints with a church.
He takes a cow and paints with a cow.
With a sardine.
With heads, hands, knives. . ."
Does not painting take in all these?

LIST OF ILLUSTRATIONS

The etchings selected from *My Life* published by Paul Cassirer, Berlin, 1922, are all approximately of the size $9\frac{1}{2} \times 7\frac{1}{2}$ in. The etchings from *Dead Souls* by Gogol, made between 1923 and 1927, are all approximately $14\frac{3}{4} \times 11$ in.

The etchings selected from La Fontaine's *Fables,* made between 1927 and 1931, are approximately $11\frac{1}{2} \times 9\frac{1}{2}$ in.

The plates taken from the Bible, made between 1931 and 1937, are all approximately $14 \times 10\frac{1}{2}$ in.

The three last books were published in Paris by Teriade (Editions Verve)

Page

19 THE STUDIO (detail)
1910; oil on canvas; $24 \times 28\frac{3}{4}$ in.; private collection

20 HOMAGE TO APOLLINAIRE, WALDEN, CENDRARS AND CANUDO
1911-12; oil on canvas; $82\frac{1}{4} \times 78$ in;
Van Abbe Museum, Eindhoven, Netherlands

21 THE WEDDING (detail)
1910-11; oil on canvas; $39\frac{1}{4} \times 74\frac{1}{4}$ in.; Chagall's collection

22 SELF-PORTRAIT WITH SEVEN FINGERS
1911; oil on canvas; $50\frac{1}{2} \times 42$ in.; Municipal Museum, Amsterdam

23 THE MOTHER AT THE STOVE
1914; oil on canvas; $25 \times 18\frac{1}{2}$ in.; private collection

24 THE MAN IN THE SNOW
1913; opaque watercolour; 12×17 in.;
Museum of Modern Art, Paris

25 THE SOLDIERS
1914; oil on canvas; $19\frac{3}{4} \times 14\frac{3}{4}$ in.; private collection

26 THE OLD MAN
1914; pen-and-ink sketch; $9\frac{7}{8} \times 6\frac{1}{4}$ in.;
private collection, Paris

27 THE LOVERS IN GREEN
1916-17; oil on canvas; $27\frac{1}{2} \times 19\frac{3}{4}$ in.; private collection

carried them to the top of a hill. (Judges 16: 1-3)
1931-37; dry-point etching for the Bible

59 THE RED HORSE
1938-44; oil on canvas; $45 \times 40\frac{1}{2}$ in.; private collection

60 THE COCK
1947; oil on canvas; $49\frac{1}{2} \times 35\frac{3}{4}$ in.; private collection

61 THE DANCE
1950-52; opaque watercolour; $25\frac{1}{2} \times 19\frac{3}{4}$ in.;
private collection

62 THE DAUGHTERS OF LOT MAKE THEIR FATHER DRINK WINE
(Genesis 19:30-36)
1931-37; dry-point etching for the Bible

63 THE MADONNA OF NOTRE DAME
1953-54; oil on canvas; $44 \times 34\frac{1}{2}$ in.; private collection

64 DAVID GIVES VENT TO HIS GRIEF
Having learnt of the death of Absolem, slain by Joab,
David gives vent to his grief. (II Samuel 18: 9-33.)
1931-37; dry-point etching for the Bible

65 THE BANKS OF THE SEINE
1953-54; oil on canvas; $31 \times 26\frac{3}{4}$ in.;
Mme. Chagall's collection

66 THE RED ROOFS
1953-54; oil on canvas; $90\frac{1}{2} \times 84$ in.; Chagall's collection

67 SUNDAY
1953-54; oil on canvas; $68 \times 58\frac{3}{4}$ in.; private collection

68 JOSEPH
Joseph at the age of seventeen, when he was feeding
the flock with his older brothers. (Genesis 37 : 2.)

69 THE CIRCUS: THE CYCLISTS
1957; oil on canvas; $60 \times 39\frac{1}{4}$ in.; private collection

70 THE LAMENTATIONS OF JEREMIAH
(Lamentations 3: 1-9.)
1931-37; dry-point etching for the Bible